ANIMALS AT RISK
GORILLAS IN DANGER

BY MICHAEL PORTMAN

Gareth Stevens
Publishing

Please visit our website, www.garethstevens.com. For a free color catalog of all our high-quality books, call toll free 1-800-542-2595 or fax 1-877-542-2596.

Library of Congress Cataloging-in-Publication Data

Portman, Michael, 1976-
Gorillas in danger / Michael Portman.
   p. cm. — (Animals at risk)
Includes index.
ISBN 978-1-4339-5796-3 (pbk.)
ISBN 978-1-4339-5797-0 (6-pack)
ISBN 978-1-4339-5794-9 (library binding)
1. Gorilla—Juvenile literature. 2. Endangered species—Juvenile literature. I. Title.
QL737.P96P668 2011
333.95'9884—dc22

          201005070

First Edition

Published in 2012 by
Gareth Stevens Publishing
111 East 14th Street, Suite 349
New York, NY 10003

Designer: Haley W. Harasymiw
Editor: Therese M. Shea

Photo credits: Cover, pp. 1, 5, 6, 7, 8, 9, 11, 15, 17, 19, 20 Shutterstock.com; p. 13 Brent Stirton/Getty Images.

Printed in the United States of America

CPSIA compliance information: Batch #CS11GS: For further information contact Gareth Stevens, New York, New York at 1-800-542-2595.

Contents

Words in the glossary appear in **bold** type the first time they are used in the text.

Gorillas are the largest **primates** in the world. They live in the forests of central Africa. There are two **species** of gorillas: eastern gorillas and western gorillas. Each species can be broken into two smaller groups, or subspecies. Eastern lowland gorillas and mountain gorillas belong to the eastern species. Western lowland gorillas and Cross River gorillas are subspecies of western gorillas.

Gorillas have few enemies in nature. However, they still face dangers. Their main **threats** are loss of their forest homes, hunters, and illness.

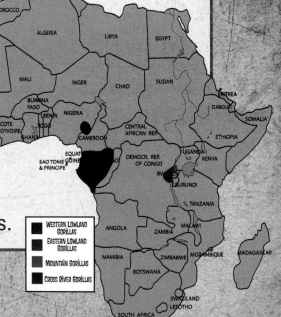

WESTERN LOWLAND GORILLAS
EASTERN LOWLAND GORILLAS
MOUNTAIN GORILLAS
CROSS RIVER GORILLAS

A gorilla's stomach is bigger than its chest.

WILD FACTS

A gorilla's arms are longer than its legs!

5

Eastern lowland gorillas are the largest gorillas. Adult males, called silverbacks, can weigh more than 500 pounds (227 kg)! Eastern lowland gorillas live only in the forests of the eastern Democratic Republic of Congo.

Like all gorillas, eastern lowland gorillas travel in groups to search for food. These groups may have as few as five or as many as thirty gorillas. They eat many kinds of plants, including leaves, stems, seeds, and tree bark. They also eat fruits and bugs.

 baby eastern lowland gorilla

▼ Eastern lowland gorillas are also called Grauer's gorillas.

WILD FACTS
Adult male gorillas have silver fur on their backs. That's why they're called "silverbacks."

An Unsafe Place

Eastern lowland gorillas live close to people. Large parts of their forest homes have been cleared for firewood and farming. This makes it harder for the gorillas to find food. In addition, there's mining in the area. The miners hunt the gorillas for meat.

The long period of war in the Democratic Republic of Congo has made it hard for people to keep eastern lowland gorillas safe. The number of eastern lowland gorillas has been falling fast. Today, there may be fewer than 5,000.

This forest has been cleared of trees, leaving no food for gorillas.

9

Mountain gorillas live in the mountains of Rwanda, Uganda, and the Democratic Republic of Congo. Mountain gorillas have very thick, long, black hair. It keeps them warm in the cold, misty air of the mountain forests.

Unlike other primates, such as orangutans, gorillas spend most of their time on the ground. However, they sometimes climb trees to look for food and to rest. Like other gorillas, mountain gorillas make nests out of leaves and branches. Sometimes they build nests in trees.

WILD FACTS

Gorillas never sleep in the same nest twice. They make a new nest each night.

Gorillas usually rest in the afternoon before looking for food again.

11

Mountain gorillas face many of the same dangers as eastern lowland gorillas. They share their mountains with Africans trying to escape war. These people are changing the forests by cutting down trees. Some also set traps to catch animals such as antelope for food. Sometimes mountain gorillas get caught instead.

People who just want to see the mountain gorillas are a danger, too. They can spread illness. Even illnesses that aren't deadly to people can kill gorillas. Today, there are only about 700 mountain gorillas left.

Officials try to keep track of the gorilla population, but they can be hard to find in thick forests.

WILD FACTS

Virunga National Park was Africa's first park. The land was set aside in 1925 to protect mountain gorillas.

Both types of western gorillas are smaller than eastern gorillas. Brown or gray hair covers their bodies. They often have reddish hair on their heads. The western lowland gorilla has the highest population of all gorillas. There are between 150,000 and 200,000 western lowland gorillas in central Africa.

Cross River gorillas live in Nigeria and Cameroon. Like western lowland gorillas, they live in thick forests. Scientists have found it hard to study these gorillas or even take photos of them. There may be fewer than 300 in all.

Gorillas have fingers much like ours. However, the primates' big toes work more like thumbs.

Western gorillas live in areas with far fewer humans than eastern gorillas. Even so, **poaching** is a serious danger. Also, businesses are cutting down trees to sell the wood. As more of the forest is cut down, it becomes easier for poachers to find the gorillas.

Illness is also a serious threat to western gorillas. **Ebola** is one of the deadliest sicknesses in the world. It can kill all kinds of primates, including people. It has killed large numbers of western lowland gorillas.

The strong muscles in a gorilla's large head help it chew.

17

Gorillas don't have babies very often. Female gorillas must be several years old before they can have babies. Once they're old enough, they'll only have a few babies in their lifetime. Gorilla babies have a high chance of dying before they're 1 year old. This makes it very hard for the population to grow.

All four subspecies of gorillas are **endangered**. So few gorillas are left that they could become extinct. Without help from people, this is a very real possibility.

This baby gorilla holds on tight while napping on its mother's back.

Luckily, there are many people helping gorillas. Wildlife **conservation** groups work with governments to protect gorillas and their **habitats**. They help create laws to stop forests from being cut down. They support groups who search the forests for poachers. They help people find food other than gorilla meat. Most importantly, they teach people about gorillas and why it's important to save them.

It's a long and hard effort, but it's not too late to save these amazing animals.

Where Gorillas Live

WESTERN GORILLAS	EASTERN GORILLAS
western lowland gorillas, Cross River gorillas	eastern lowland gorillas, mountain gorillas
Nigeria	Rwanda
Cameroon	Uganda
Gabon	Democratic Republic of Congo
Democratic Republic of Congo	
Republic of Congo	
Central African Republic	
Angola	
Equatorial Guinea	

GLOSSARY

conservation: the protection of the natural world

Ebola: a disease that causes high fever, headache, muscle aches, and bleeding, and often results in death

endangered: in danger of dying out

extinct: having no living members

habitat: an area where plants, animals, or other living things live

poaching: illegal hunting

primate: a member of the group of animals that includes people, monkeys, gorillas, and chimpanzees

species: a group of animals that are all of the same kind

threat: something likely to cause harm

For More Information

Books

Nichols, Michael. *Face to Face with Gorillas.* Washington, DC: National Geographic Children's Books, 2009.

Pimm, Nancy Roe. *The Heart of the Beast: Eight Great Gorilla Stories.* Plain City, OH: Darby Creek Publishing, 2007.

Websites

Gorillas
wwf.panda.org/what_we_do/endangered_species/great_apes/gorillas/
Read about gorillas and learn how you can help them.

Mammals: Gorilla
www.sandiegozoo.org/animalbytes/t-gorilla.html
Read fun facts about gorillas and see photos of them in action.

INDEX